How to Grow Rich with The Power of Compounding

Accelerated Wealth Creation Blueprint, for the Success you truly deserve!

By

Praveen Kumar & Prashant Kumar

©Copyright 2018 By Praveen Kumar

Terms of Use

This Electronic book is Copyright © 2018 By Praveen Kumar. All rights are reserved. No part of this book may be reproduced, stored in a retrieval system, or transmitted by any means; electronic, mechanical, photocopying, recording, or otherwise, without written permission from the copyright holder(s).

Disclaimer

The advice contained in this material might not be suitable for everyone. The author obtained the information from sources believed to be reliable and from his own personal experience, but he neither implies nor intends any guarantee of accuracy.

The author, publisher and distributors never give legal, accounting, medical or any other type of professional advice. The reader must always seek those services from competent professionals that can review their own particular circumstances.

The author, publisher and distributors particularly disclaim any liability, loss, or risk taken by individuals who directly or indirectly act on the information contained herein. All readers must accept full responsibility for their use of this material.

All pictures used in this book are for illustrative purposes only. The people in the pictures are not connected with the book, author or publisher and no link or endorsement between any of them and the topic or content is implied, nor should any be assumed. The pictures are only licensed for use in this book and must not be used for any other purpose without prior written permission of the rights holder.

Table of contents

UNDERSTANDING THE POWER OF COMPOUNDING 1

THE TUNNELING EFFECT 5

COMPOUNDING WORKS IN TIME 9

STUDY BY MARKET LOGIC 11

EFFECT OF A SMALL INCREASE IN INTEREST RATE 19

HOW A SINGLE DOLLAR HAS THE POWER TO GROW INTO A MILLION DOLLARS 21

HOW A DOLLAR A DAY WILL MAKE YOU A MILLIONAIRE IN YOUR LIFETIME 23

COMPOUNDING IN REVERSE - CAN MAKE YOU GO BROKE 27

HOW TO FIND DOLLARS TO INVEST AND COMPOUND? 29

FIVE STEPS TO HARNESS THE POWER OF COMPOUNDING 41

WHAT ABOUT INFLATION? 43

OTHER BOOKS BY THE AUTHORS 53

ABOUT THE AUTHORS 55

Albert Einstein, arguably one of the smartest men to have lived, is reputed to have said, "The most powerful force in the universe is compound interest." He called it the "***Eight Wonder of the World***". However, it is baffling that so few of us fully comprehend the dynamics of compounding, its application and the paramount power it generates. We were taught how to solve compounding problems at school—and back then we were completely oblivious to its awesome power... Our teachers would have been millionaires had they understood its power. Unfortunately, like us, they only knew how to solve textual problems without being fully aware of the magnitude of it; when applied correctly- it has the capacity to change our financial future.

Understanding the Power of Compounding

For the ease of understanding let us take an example: Imagine you could invest one dollar at the beginning of the month—now imagine that one dollar in saving double with each passing day for an entire month.

On day two your investment will double to $2, on day three it will be $4 and on day four it will amount to $8, so on and so forth. I have plotted weekly graphs below to show you how your investment will increase. Allow these graphs to impinge on your mind, heart and soul because they hold the fundamental principle for you to become rich.

First Week

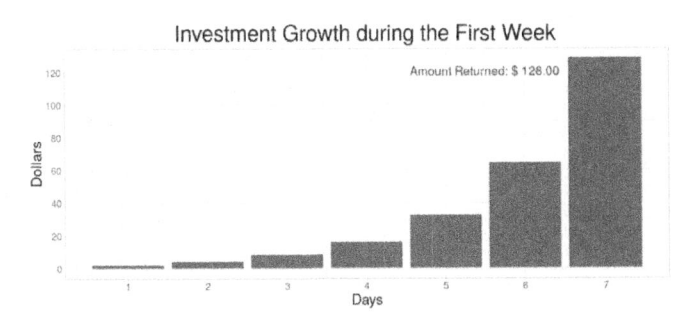

If you observe the graph above, you will notice that on day seven your initial investment will be worth $128. Nothing too inspiring, right?

Second Week - After the end of two weeks (fourteen days-see graph below) your investment would have increased to $16,384. I'm sure it is still not exhilarating. .

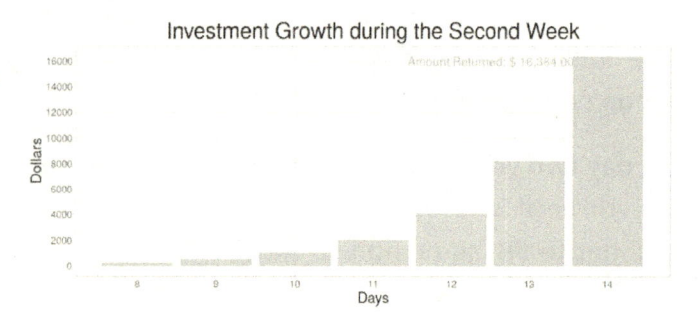

Investment Growth during the Second Week

Third Week

On completion of three weeks (21 days), your investment would have grown to over two million as depicted in the graph below. Now things are starting to get interesting.

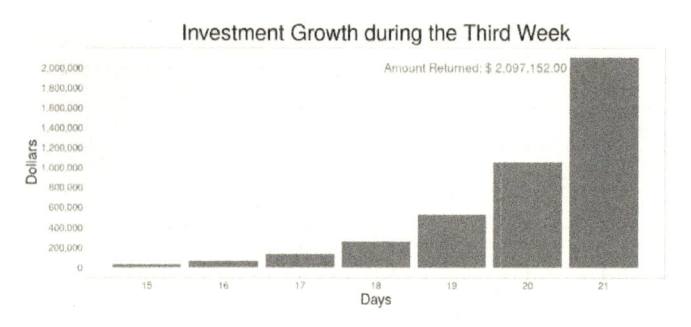

Investment Growth during the Third Week

Last 10 Days

At the end of four weeks (28 days), your one-dollar investment will now be worth over two hundred and sixty eight million dollars. Wow, this is getting interesting.

The fun is not over. In the next three days: 29th, 30th and 31st, your net worth will be over two billion dollars ($2,147,483,648, to be exact). In the last three days your investment multiplies nearly 10 fold. See how your money increases in a matter of four days (28th-31st), on the chart below.

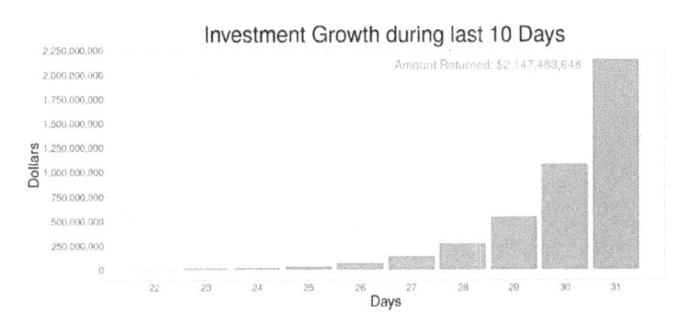

Investment Growth during last 10 Days
Amount Returned: $2,147,483,648

Graph Depicting the Entire Month's Growth

To help put your investment into perspective–observe the graph below that depicts how your investment will grow during the month. You will notice that during the initial period (up to the 22nd day, to be precise) your growth is not even visible on the chart. This is called the *'Tunneling Effect'* that I will describe in the succeeding paragraph.

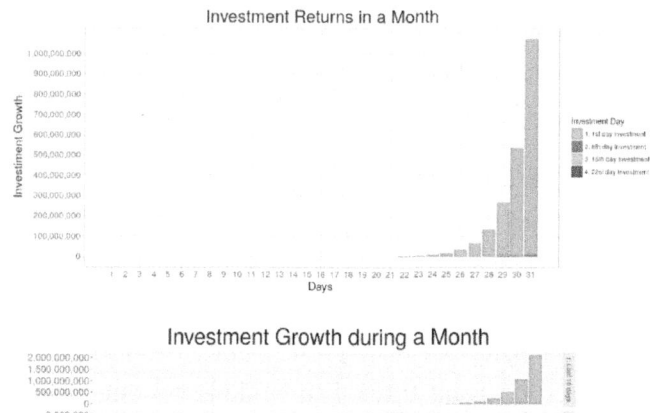

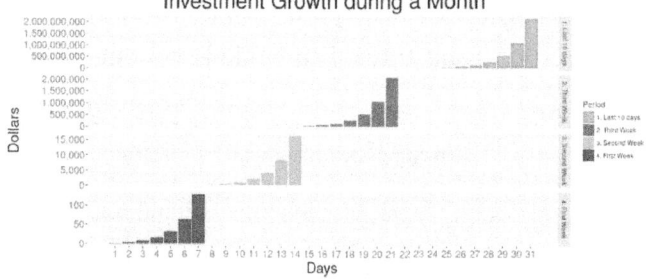

Investment Returns in a Month

Investment Growth during a Month

These graphs have been included to highlight the simple truth that "With compounding your money multiplies exponentially if you give it time."

If you were to wait just one more day—that is the first day of the following month, then your net worth will double to $4.3 billion. Moving forward with the passage of each successive day, your net worth will continue to expand at a mind-boggling pace.

The Tunneling Effect

When you first start out investing using compound interest, all the hard work takes place upfront, in the beginning. You have nothing to show for your effort.

This is called the 'Tunneling Effect'; it causes a lot of dismay and most people give up at this point because they do not see any tangible results for their sacrifice, hard work and effort.

If there is a confluence of patience and perseverance at this stage, then there is not only light at the end of the tunnel—there's an illuminating Sun shining in all its glory for you to bask in. Anyone who has become wealthy has passed through this dark tunnel. There is no escaping it.

"Nothing in the world can take the place of persistence. Talent will not; nothing is more common than unsuccessful men of talent. Genius will not; unrewarded genius is almost a proverb. Education will not; the world is full of educated derelicts. Persistence and determination alone are omnipotent."

~ Calvin Coolidge

Warren Buffet, one of the richest men in the world, remarked about his wife when he was building his wealth "***Susie didn't get very excited when I told her we were going to get rich. She either didn't care or didn't believe me - probably both, in fact.***" You can read the biography of any wealth creator, and you will find in it the universal truth of the 'tunneling effect' and how they wanted to quit but didn't.

Critical Mass

If you persist and as the time goes on the critical mass kicks in and things begin to get better. Your investment becomes self-perpetuating; it starts growing under its own steam. The challenge at this stage is to not change course

The problem with the human mind is that it loses its focus rather easily; it diverts its attention to other thoughts and ideas. It will eventually start looking at other options. The key here is to maintain focus. Compounding is boring— B-O-R-I-N-G. It is boring until the money starts to pour in; compounding becomes very interesting hereon. In fact, it becomes downright fascinating! Compounding, if allowed to continue, catalyzes the expansion of your wealth to unfathomable levels.

The principle of compounding is also applicable to other forms of investment like: real estate investments and network marketing. Ninety percent of people drop out of network marketing because they do not fully appreciate the power of compounding. They feel discouraged once they face, and have to endure that tunneling effect, and quit. They fail to see the light that is just around the corner; dogged persistence is a great quality to have if you want to succeed.

Compounding Works in Time

The great thing about compounding is that anyone can do it. Compounding is the royal road to riches. Compounding is the safe road and the sure road. To compound successfully you need the following: **perseverance** in order to keep you firm on the savings path and you need **time**—time to allow the power of compounding to work for you. **Time, in fact, is the most powerful element in the process of compounding; nothing comes close to it.**

There is a paragraph in *'The Richest Man in Babylon, The Power of Time'* that explains this perfectly:

"Wealth, like a tree, grows from a tiny seed. The first copper you save is the seed from which your tree of wealth shall grow. The sooner you plant that seed, the sooner shall the tree grow. And the more faithfully you nourish and water that tree with consistent savings, the sooner may you bask in contentment beneath its shade" (George S. Clason, 1926).

Study by Market Logic

In order to emphasize the importance of time in the power of compounding, I am including this extraordinary study done by *Market Logic*, of Ft. Lauderdale, FL 33306.

In this study we assume that investor B opens an IRA at age 19. For seven consecutive periods, he puts $2,000 in his IRA at an average growth rate of 10% (7% interest plus growth). After seven years, this fellow makes NO MORE contributions—he's finished.

A second investor, A, makes no contributions until age 26 (this is the age when investor B was finished with his contributions). Then A continues faithfully to contribute $2,000 every year till he turns 65 (at the same theoretical 10% rate).

Now study these incredible results: B, who started investing at an earlier age and who made only seven contributions, ends up with MORE money than A, who made 40 contributions but at a LATER TIME. The difference in the two is that *B had seven additional years of compounding than A*; those seven early years were worth more than all of A's 33 supplementary contributions.

I exhort you to introduce this study to your kids. It reiterates the fact that the earlier you start, the richer you will be.

	INVESTOR A		INVESTOR B	
Age	Contribution	Year-End Value	Contribution	Year-End Value
8	0	0	0	0
9	0	0	0	0
10	0	0	0	0
11	0	0	0	0
12	0	0	0	0
13	0	0	0	0
14	0	0	0	0
15	0	0	0	0
16	0	0	0	0
17	0	0	0	0
18	0	0	0	0
19	0	0	2,000	2,200
20	0	0	2,000	4,620
21	0	0	2,000	7,282
22	0	0	2,000	10,210

How to Grow Rich with The Power of Compounding

23	0	0	2,000	13,431
24	0	0	2,000	16,974
25	0	0	2,000	20,872
26	2,000	2,200	0	22,959
27	2,000	4,620	0	25,255
28	2,000	7,282	0	27,780
29	2,000	10,210	0	30,558
30	2,000	13,431	0	33,614
31	2,000	16,974	0	36,976
32	2,000	20,872	0	40,673
33	2,000	25,139	0	44,741
34	2,000	29,875	0	49,215
35	2,000	35,062	0	54,136
36	2,000	40,769	0	59,550
37	2,000	47,045	0	65,505
38	2,000	53,950	0	72,055
39	2,000	61,545	0	79,261
40	2,000	69,899	0	87,187
41	2,000	79,089	0	95,905
42	2,000	89,198	0	105,496
43	2,000	100,318	0	116,045
44	2,000	112,550	0	127,650
45	2,000	126,005	0	140,415

46	2,000	140,805	0	154,456
47	2,000	157,086	0	169,902
48	2,000	174,995	0	186,892
49	2,000	194,694	0	205,581
50	2,000	216,364	0	226,140
51	2,000	240,200	0	248,754
52	2,000	266,420	0	273,629
53	2,000	295,262	0	300,992
54	2,000	326,988	0	331,091
55	2,000	361,887	0	364,200
56	2,000	400,276	0	400,620
57	2,000	442,503	0	440,682
58	2,000	488,953	0	484,750
59	2,000	540,049	0	533,225
60	2,000	596,254	0	586,548
61	2,000	658,079	0	645,203
62	2,000	726,087	0	709,723
63	2,000	800,896	0	780,695
64	2,000	883,185	0	858,765
65	2,000	973,704	0	944,641

Less Total Invested:	**80,000**	**14,000**
Equal Net Earnings:	**893,704**	**930,641**

| Money Grew: | 11-fold | 66-fold |

Remember that as time passes, the power of compounding accelerates dramatically. If you're a young person, all you need to know is that you must start early to stay ahead in the game of compounding and wealth creation. The best time to plant a seed was twenty years ago; now is your second opportunity to do the same. Do not waste a day!

Some Fun Math

Let us take an example of Kid A, who gets a supposedly great paying job for a 20-year-old at 45k per annum. He actually survives on the same 15k a year that Kid B, going to med-school, survived on. Now let's assume that the 20-year-old who skipped med-school for that great paying job invested the remaining 30k of his salary in stocks.

Here are the facts:

The med-school student, Kid B, graduates 'on time' at the age of 28; secures a job paying 75k a year and pays all of his debts off by the age of 33— so theoretically, he's 33 before he actually has an effective salary of 75k.

Kid A, who skipped med-school and invested in stocks, earned the historical average of 10.1% annually on his money (10.1% since 1926...but if you skip the Great Depression years the average is actually closer to 13%). So, where is this kid at the age of 33? He has $920,180 dollars in compounding assets. Coupled with his 45k annual salary, he will earn 135k at the age of 33 while the doctor earns 75k.

The doctor cannot mathematically catch up to the scrub (Kid A) who's still at his 45k year salary (maybe more). 13 years hence, he has about 122k to reinvest in the market that year while the doctor will never be able to match that investment; he will always play the catch-up game no matter how much he may earn.

But none of this actually happens, does it? That kid, A doesn't invest, and the doctor stays in debt. The statistics mentioned above are just used as a guide to elucidate a point; it does not mean that the right education doesn't give fruitful results. There are better chances of a financially educated person investing than a college drop out.

What's the point?

The point is that understanding compounding and starting out early makes you wealthy. It's surprising they don't teach real-life economics in school.

The Golden Rule of Accumulation is – START EARLY. Time, without a doubt, is the most important powerful weapon in an investor's arsenal. There is nothing that comes close to it.

"When you're young, you have an asset money can't buy: TIME. Start saving now and turn pocket change into riches." (Erin Burt, 2007)

The power of compounding accelerates and creates a snowball of money. At first, your returns may appear unsatisfactory, but if you're patient, eventually, your initial investment will grow enormously.

Effect of a Small Increase in Interest Rate

Another important facet of compounding is that a small change in the rate of return can produce a huge impact over time. For instance, if you gift your newborn son $10,000, and if his portfolio returns 10% annually, then your original gift of $10,000 will grow to $4.5 million by the time he is 65. But if his portfolio returns 8%, then it grows to only $1.4 million. On the other hand, if it returns only 5%, the portfolio will increase to a mere $227,000. In other words, if the rate of return is halved then, the portfolio will be less than 1/20th the size.

This is a very crucial to remember—a minimal percentage change in interest rate can have a huge impact on the final outcome. So, when you are investing or borrowing money for real estate/business, negotiate interest to the second decimal point. Banks and financial institutions understand this because it is their bread and butter. So should you, because if you do not negotiate hard no one will give you an inch. In the game of money, he wins who understands money the best.

How a Single Dollar Has the Power to Grow into a Million Dollars

Every dollar bill is a money seed. Like any seed, if it is planted and allowed to grow it becomes a money tree. This tree once grown up will bear fruit year after year. It will also provide with the seeds necessary to plant further trees. If you destroy the seed, it will never grow to be a tree. Now let us see how the one-dollar seed grows into a million-dollar tree.

If you invest one dollar at 5% rate of interest, it would grow into a million-dollar tree in 284 years. If the same dollar is invested at 10% interest rate the time is cut short to 145 years. It will take only 75 years for a dollar to become a million if you invested at 20%. Not planning to live that long? Then plant a few more dollar bills. It is that simple. Let us see what happens if you start planting one dollar every day, i.e. $30 in a month.

How a Dollar a Day will make you a Millionaire in your Lifetime

It is easy if you want to become a millionaire in your lifetime then save one dollar a day and invest it sensibly. Please study the following statements carefully:

A dollar a day invested at 5% will take 100 years to become a million.

A dollar a day invested at 10% will take 56 years to become a million.

A dollar a day invested at 20% will make you a millionaire in only 32 years.

Want to be a billionaire? A dollar a day, when compounded at 20% interest, will give you a billionaire in 66 years.

You will say that earning 20% return is not possible. Later in this book, I will show you how you can receive not only 20%, but go as high as 60% to 70% or even a 100% return on your investment.

This magic happens if you plant one dollar bills every day. I am reasonably sure that most of us can do better than $30 a month. We can dramatically cut short the period and become millionaires much faster if we can plant let us say $10 seeds every day.

If you understand this simple mathematics, then that one dollar bill in your hands will never feel the same again. It holds the seed for your financial future and wellbeing. If you lose it or spend it foolishly, then the dollar seed is destroyed forever. If you save it and invest it wisely, it has the potential to make you and your family rich forever. Once it grows into a million-dollar tree—it will bear that fruit for you and your family, year after year.

You will ask if making a million dollars is so simple then why is not everyone a millionaire. The simple answer to that is lack of discipline. Most people lack the discipline and perseverance required over an extended period of time.

Becoming a millionaire can be a very boring and repetitive exercise over a period of time. Most people want excitement and thrill, and in the process, they gamble away their financial future.

There will be sceptics who will say sustained 20% growth is not possible. Well, Warren Buffet, the investment guru, has done it consecutively for the past 40 years for his investors.

Later in this book, you will see strategies that can help you grow at a much faster rate than 20%. You don't need to be a financial genius to achieve this. All you need are a few financial skills and discipline. Justly put, all you need to do is funnel some of your ill-spent dollars into financially sound investments.

Compounding in Reverse - Can Make You Go Broke

The power of compounding works both ways. It can also make you bankrupt. For compounding to work in your favor, you must always spend less than what you earn and invest the difference. When you invest the difference, money starts working for you. It works day and night, twenty-four hours, seven days a week whether you sleep or go on a holiday. As time goes by and as you have more and more money working for you a day comes when you stop working for money.

On the other hand moment, you start spending more than you earn, you are forced to borrow money, and that generally comes at interest. The reverse power of compounding then kicks in. Unfortunately, most people fail to fully understand this reverse power of compound interest. They max out their credit cards. The effective cost of borrowings in most cases is more than 20% and at times over 30%. The result is that they go into a tailspin and go bust.

There is an old adage, *"He who understands interest – earns it. He who doesn't understand*

interest – pays it. " Be the one who earns interest than the one who pays interest.

How to find Dollars to Invest and Compound?

Saving is the Key to Compounding

You can never build the wealth you desire if you do not spend less than what you earn and learn to invest the difference. In the majority of the cases, the rich are not rich because they earn a lot of money. The rich are rich because they save a lot of money and invest.

Compounding principle is not possible if you spend more than you earn. Even if your salary is a million dollar and you spend million plus one-dollar compounding will simply not work.

The only way you can find dollars to invest is either by increasing your earning power or simplifying your life to reduce your spending.

In the beginning, it is far easier to understand and make changes to your spending habits.

For those living on subsistence level, it may not be possible to change their spending habits by very much because most of their purchases are for necessities of life.

There are however leaks that occur in our spending of which we are sometimes not even aware of. If we can stop the leaks and save a few dollars each day then we can generate funds for investing and be on our way to becoming millionaires. Please find below some suggestions that can generate instant cash flow for investing:

1. Think before you buy – Every time you make a purchase take an extra minute, to think if you really need to buy that item. Rich take that extra one minute and poor don't. Most of the time we buy on impulse and get saddled with unnecessary things that we don't need in our lives. Think also if you can rent an item or borrow it from somewhere if you don't need it for long. These can include renting a DVD or getting a book from the library instead of buying it.

2. Delayed Gratification – This is true for luxury items. Just delay the purchase by a couple of months. If you want to buy a new car, delay it. If you want to purchase a TV, just delay it by a year. This simple act of delaying purchases will add thousands of dollars to your pocket.

3. Increase your Planning Horizon – By only increasing your planning horizon you can save hundreds of dollars. As with airline tickets, the longer the planning horizon, the cheaper the purchase.

4. Ask for a discount – If you don't request a discount, you will never get one. Always ask for one! You will be surprised how many times you will get one. Remember every dollar saved is a potential million-dollar tree.

5. Examine the Receipt for Errors – Always ask for a receipt and examine it for errors. This simple act will save you hundreds of dollars every year for planting seeds for the money tree.

6. File your Receipts – You must file your receipts as soon as you get back home. This serves two purposes. Firstly, you can change or replace an item if it does not work or becomes faulty. Secondly, you can claim a tax rebate if you are self-employed or running a business. Most people throw the receipt, misplace it or dump it into a cardboard box from where it is troublesome to retrieve at the time of filing tax return. If you are in 30% tax bracket- you lose 30% money on each and every receipt you misplace. It may look minor but is a huge loss when you consider it from the point of destroying seeds that would have made you millions of dollars in potential income.

7. Plug in Tax Leaks - What most people do not realize is that the biggest chunk of cash outflow from their pocket is their taxes. These can range anywhere from 20% to 55% of the income. This is huge in terms of dollars. Most people hesitate in employing the services of a competent tax consultant, thinking that it costs money. Nothing can be further from truth. A good tax consultant, through his advice on tax planning, will not only pay for his services but also save you thousands of dollars that can be used for planting money trees. Another suggestion is that even if you are a paid employee, you should think in terms of starting a home business or invest in property to save on tax. Please speak with your local tax consultant before you embark on this course because tax laws are different in each country.

8. Buying Wholesale– Avoid paying retail price for your purchases. Try and buy at wholesale prices or at stores that offer discounts. Use coupons, shop online and compare prices. Make this a habit. It will save you thousands of dollars every year on your primary purchases.

9. Carryout Plastic Surgery – Want to save 20% to 30% in your expenses? Take out all the credit cards from your wallet or purse and cut all the cards except one. Make it a habit to pay off your credit card balance as and when the payment is due. Never pay the minimum balance. It is the costliest loan you will ever borrow. With the use of plastic credit cards we have lost the feel of money. It does not hurt to spend money because we don't see it coming out of our wallet. Buying now and paying later creates a cycle of debt. Instead, we should save now and invest in the future. These simple actions will set you free and save you massively—up to 30 percent in the coming year.

10. Check your Automatic Payments – These days, for the sake of convenience, we set up automatic payments for all our regular expenses. We set payments for our electricity bills, insurance, water bills, rates, hire purchases, mortgage payment, telephone bills, credit card payments, etc. on monthly or weekly basis. If counted this is a massive financial outflow from our pocket. The danger here is that once we set up the automatic payment, we tend to forget about it and fail to regularly audit our cash outflow. We do not analyze our bills. We become complacent and never shop around for new mortgages or insurance even when there are cheaper products available. Regular auditing of your automatic payments is an absolute must if you desire to save dollars for investment seeds.

11. Energy Audit – Energy costs are soaring. They are likely to increase further in the coming years. Our energy bills, whether it is the cost of heating, cooling, lighting, cooking or driving a car will form a fundamental part of our expense basket. It is imperative that we take a hard look at this major source of outflow of our hard-earned money. Most energy companies will carry out an energy audit of your home for free. You must take advantage of these audits and consider technological measures to reduce your long-term energy bills, and make changes to your house, living style and the kind of car you drive—this will not only save you hundreds of dollars every year but also save the environment.

12. Buy Second-Hand – You can save thousands of dollars by buying second-hand. For instance, a new car out of the showroom drops in price by around 20 percent. It is prudent to buy a second-hand car that is one to three-years old, which can be purchased at a discount of 20 percent to 50 percent on the original purchase price. A dollar saved is a dollar earned! — And you are on your way to planting money seeds.

13. Make a Garage Sale – Look around your house and storage. You will find hundreds of items that have outlived their utility for you. Be it a piece of furniture, some book or baby clothes you no longer need. These may be handy items for someone who needs them. Carry out a garage sale or list them on an internet site that specializes in such sales. You will not only clear your house of unnecessary junk but will also generate invaluable dollar seeds that can get you started on the path to become a millionaire.

14. Barter Your Skills – You can save hundreds of dollars by trading your skills; by becoming a member of exchanges that are springing up in most towns and countries. This was the oldest form of business before money was invented and is again gaining popularity. This can be a source of considerable savings in your travel, entertainment and repair bills if you are willing to exchange your skills.

15. Hundreds of Other Creative Ways – There are hundreds of other ways to save money. You are only limited by your imagination. Dine out? Eat in. Use carpool to work. Take the bus instead of a cab. Email instead of using the phone. Go out for a swim in the sea or for a picnic in the park—it is free entertainment. Never buy extra service contracts or extended warranties; manufacturing guarantees are in most cases adequate. Only run a full dish washer. Put on warm clothing instead of room heating. Take a shower instead of a bath. Don't play lottery, casino or go to races— the law of probability insinuates that you will always be a big loser. The list is as big as your imagination. If you take action on even few of the suggestions, you will have more than enough dollar seeds to plant and to become a millionaire.

What is the Right Philosophy?

Many will say, 'why must I plant dollar seeds for the future? Let me live in the present and be merry. Who has seen the future? It is the present that matters.'

The problem with this philosophy is that you will continue to work for money. There will be no respite for you even in your old age, when you want to slow down and be looked after. Your money problems will continue to haunt you. The 'pleasure-now' philosophy is full of ugly potholes.

On the other hand, if you take the trouble of making some changes as suggested in the above paragraphs and start planting dollar seeds then your life will change as soon as the compounding kicks in, and the dollar tree becomes big and powerful. It will also start giving more seeds and as a result, start multiplying further. The money then starts working for you, and you will find financial freedom.

How much to spend? How much to save and invest for the future? Those are profoundly philosophical questions. Each one of us has to find the right balance that is correct our family and us at a particular point in life. But whatever the situation in life, we have to find dollar seeds to plant or our lives will never change for the better.

The Rule of 72

An easy method to calculate compound interest problems in your head is by applying the Rule of 72.

By using this rule, you can find the number of years that are needed to double your money at a given interest rate—you simply divide 72 by the interest rate!

For example, if you wish to find out how long it will take to double your money at 8% interest then divide 72 by 8, and the answer is that it will take 9 years to double your money.

The rule of 72 is very accurate, as long as the rate of interest is less than 20%.

You can also run the problem backwards. If you want to find out at what rate of interest you will double your money in, let us say, 6 years. To get the answer all you need to do is dividing 72 by 6. The answer, in this case, is 12% interest.

Procrastination

You must stop fretting and procrastinating in case you have lost a lot of investing time. There is nothing you can do about it. It is water under the bridge. There is no point in thinking or complaining about the past. Think about the future. You need to start today, right now, this very second! There is no time to waste. You can make a difference to your finances by making an investment today. Twenty years from now, you'll be glad you did.

Procrastination is the natural assassin of opportunity. Every day you delay in investing makes your ultimate goal of financial freedom at risk.

"Every gold piece you save is a slave to work for you. Every copper it earns is its child that also can earn for you. If you would become wealthy, then what you save must earn, and its children must earn, that all may help to give to you the abundance you crave" (George Samuel Clason, 1926).

The Cost of Waiting One Year

It's human nature to procrastinate and waste valuable time. Most people do not have a plan for savings. Even if they do have one, they say, "I will start saving next year" or "I'll do it later." Little do they realize that the costs of delaying are enormous? Even one year can make a huge difference.

Let me illustrate this with an example; let us say that Tom makes $5,000 annual contributions to a retirement fund that earns him an 8% return. He'll have $1,932,528.09 saved by retirement. In case he waits, let us say, by five years, his annual contributions would have to increase to nearly $7,500 to save that same amount by age 65.

Five Steps to Harness the Power of Compounding

There are four steps you need to take to harness the power of compound interest to work for you.

•Spend Less than What You Earn. This is the starting point. Whatever your income level, at any point in life, you have to spend less than what you earn and invest the difference to apply the power and enjoy the benefits of compounding. If you spend more than you earn, then you will delve into the tailspin of reverse compounding with disastrous financial results.

•Start Young. The earlier you start, the more time compounding will have to work in your favor, as illustrated through the examples taken up previously, the wealthier you will become. ***The next best thing to starting young is starting now.***

•Make Regular Investments. Remember that even a little investment goes a long way. You have to remain disciplined and make saving a priority. Do whatever it takes to maximize your contributions.

•**Be Patient.** Do not touch the money. You will be tempted several times. Resist. Compounding only works with time, provided you allow your investment to grow. The results will seem slow at first but persevere. The magic of compounding returns shows at the very end. You have to be patient for compounding to work its awesome power.

***Interest Rate**. Always negotiate the best interest rate. Even a small change in rate of return will work like magic to the final outcome and your financial security.

What about inflation?

Most people will argue that $1 million will not have the same purchasing power in 40 years as it has today. This is absolutely true. This is all the more reason for you to start saving now! Over the years your income will also begin to rise. With each increase in your income, if you will increase your investment, then you will add more fuel to the fire of compounding and be on the path of becoming really rich.

Having a couple of million bucks in 40 years is better than not having any money at all. Start as soon as possible and invest what you can to let the power of compounding work its magic.

Leveraging For Higher Returns

The best part is you don't have to wait for years for the power of compounding to work if you apply it the phenomenal power of leveraging.

Archimedes used to say "**Give me a place to stand and with a lever I will move the whole world**." This illustrates the awesome power of leverage. Big doors swing on little hinges. Leverage is the power to achieve a lot with little or no effort.

To create wealth in large amount in quick time one has to understand and master the principle of leverage. Correct application of leverage breaks through the barrier of 10% growth/ yield. With leverage we can grow at 50% or 60% and even 100% or more.

Leverage when combined with the principle of compounding can create accelerated wealth. No great wealth has ever been created without using either leverage or compounding. The two when combined together can explode your wealth. Let us examine how leverage works in the financial world.

Other People's Money

Whether you are in business or an investor funds are needed to grow. Everyone starts with personal funds but these run out sooner than later. To create wealth one has to borrow from relatives, friends, banks, financial institutions or public. In other words we have to work with **'Other People's Money'** or **OPM**.

The borrowed funds have to be productively employed so as to earn higher return than the interest payable. Banks do this all the time. They borrow money from us at a lower interest rate and then give out loans to businesses and property mortgages at a much higher interest rate. They pocket the difference and create millions of dollars in profit. To create wealth we have to think like a bank. We have to use Other People's Money to grow.

To explain this point let us see how leverage works in real estate. Let us say you buy an investment property for $100,000 with 10% down payment. This means that you make a down payment of $10,000 and borrow $90,000 from the bank. Let us assume that the rent from the property covers the interest and expenses on the property. If the value of the property increases by 7% in the year then the property would be worth $107,000. This would mean that your investment of $10,000 has earned whopping return of $7000 or 70% yield. This happens because you get to leverage not only on your investment of $10,000 but also on the borrowed amount of $90,000.

There are sophisticated property investors who buy property with 'no money down'or very little of their own money i.e. they work on 100% borrowed funds. In this case the return on investment will be infinity.

You can use leverage in share, forex or commodity trading. You can also apply leveraging in your business if you have one. Network marketing works on the principle of leveraging.

Borrowing money and creating debt is good if the funds are utilized intelligently to create wealth through business and investment. The profits need to exceed the cost of borrowing.

A debt created for consumption purposes for buying luxury items are bad debts. These debts take money out of our pockets and have to be treated with great caution. Good debts make us rich. Poor debts make us go broke. The power of leverage in finance when applied correctly can make us grow rich exponentially.

Caution about Leveraging

Leveraging is a great way of creating accelerated wealth but it comes with a warning. If leveraging is applied incorrectly it can destroy your wealth equally fast. Leverage works both ways. It is a double edged sword.

The financial crisis of 2008 was caused when excessive greed led people to use leverage without proper understanding of risks involved. **The most important factor for using leverage correctly is your state of knowledge**. For instance if you lack knowledge about finances or the business/investment you wish to start there is no point in rushing to get a 100% finance in order try a do a no money down deal. Stay away from leveraging if you do not have knowledge about the product or service you are investing in.

Before applying leverage you have to access your risk appetite. This is because if things go wrong then people with less risk appetite will start to panic and make wrong financial decisions that can set them back by years in their financial growth and planning.

If you are using leverage for accelerated financial return then you have to be very alert towards changing market conditions. If the market conditions deteriorate then you have to take measures to reduce your leverage in time. People go bankrupt when they hesitate to act or foresee a developing situation. Reducing your leverage by selling some of your assets is no shame. You can always buy assets and increase your leverage when favorable market conditions return.

You should make a correct assessment of your financial, emotional and spiritual intelligence in any given situation before applying leverage as an instrument for accelerated wealth creation. Greed is a product of lack of emotional and spiritual intelligence. Leverage driven by greed is the worst enemy of wealth creation.

Leverage is like a power tool that can make your job of wealth creation very easy but its improper use without adequate knowledge or precautions can cause you tremendous hurt.

The above arguments should not dissuade you from using leverage with prudence and intelligence. This is the most important and powerful tool in the armory of wealth creators. However, it is of paramount importance to understand its correct usage before applying it in a fit of excitement. Initially start applying small forms of leverage and as your confidence grows you can increase the amount of leverage you are comfortable with.

Remember without applying some kind of leverage there is no possibility of creating accelerated wealth.

Compounding + Leveraging = Accelerated Growth

Final Thoughts

So, let us recoup: the power of compounding can make any disciplined and prudent man into a millionaire, there is no extra ordinary skill or genius required and any ordinary man or woman can achieve the desired result.

The ability to save and invest is the key to becoming rich. Obviously, a high income helps. The only proven method is to let your investments compound. Higher the return, faster your wealth will grow. Even modest savings will produce a golden nest egg that you can hatch later in life.

Miracle of compounding which wise men refer to as the 'Eighth Wonder' is a sure and slow path to great wealth. It magically turns a small amount of money, invested wisely, into a whole lot of cash.

Always remember that every dollar that you earn or save, is a seed that has the potential to make a million Dollars for you. So, look after each dollar seed and plant them carefully, and make them grow into trees. They will bear fruits for your family, for generations to come and set you on the path of financial freedom.

The only action required is to find dollar seeds and to continue planting them. If you take the initial steps, remain focused and persist whilst facing the 'Tunneling Effect,' then one day, the power of compounding will take over and become self-perpetuating to take you to the destination of untold riches.

You don't need to be a genius to harness the Power of Compounding to grow rich. This is no rocket science. It is the simplest and most B-O-R-I-N-G way of becoming wealthier. The only thing needed to compound your money successfully is a 100% commitment.

Each dollar that you have is a seed that can be planted to earn you hundreds of dollars. These, in turn, can be planted to earn thousands and millions of dollars.

The Power of Compounding is akin to a snowball…roll it down a snowy hill, and it'll build on itself to grow bigger and bigger. Before you know it, there will be an avalanche of money.

GET THE BALL ROLLING! DON'T WASTE A SINGLE MINUTE!

The time it takes to compound is a function of the amount of money (dollar seeds) you invest, and at what interest rate. We have seen that a small change in interest rate can make a huge change to the final outcome.

It gets even more exciting when the power of compounding is used with the power of leveraging for accelerated wealth creation.

The purpose of this book will be served if it helps in educating and help morph enlightened people who create wealth the right way, preserve wealth the right way and ultimately, use their wealth for the greater good of humanity. This process leads to seeking a higher purpose in life and its fulfillment. I hope and pray that to some extent, that purpose is served. If you have read to this point, I thank you with gratitude in my heart and hope you succeed in creating true wealth that helps not only you and your family but entire humanity.

If you liked the book and gained some knowledge that will be useful to you in life, then please leave an honest review to help others find this book. It will be a small effort on your part, but an act of charity that may help in changing few lives for the better. We thank you in advance for your help.

This book is about fundamental principles of wealth creation that can be applied to any business or investing strategy. At [Wealth Creation Academy](), we teach multitude ways to generate passive income, which includes: real estate investing, digital publishing, affiliate marketing, multi-level marketing and investing in forex, commodities, and shares by copying experienced traders that need very little of time. You may like to get started with some of the strategies depending on your budget and time.

Other Books by the Authors

Praveen Kumar has authored several bestselling books. Please visit his website **http://praveenkumarauthor.com/** for more information

About the Authors

Praveen Kumar was abandoned by his father at the age of fourteen and joined the Navy at tender age of fifteen where education, roof and free food were guaranteed.

In order to understand the root cause of suffering he turned towards philosophy and religion. After 10 years of soul searching and meditation he understood that 'life is 'and material and spiritual world are closely interwoven. You cannot live in one without the other.

Praveen was highly successful in the Navy, where he successfully commanded submarines, sailed around the world in a yacht and received gallantry award for his contribution to the Navy.

Despite his success in the Navy, Praveen realized that lack of financial security for his family was one of key root causes of his suffering, resulting from his childhood deprivation. To improve his financial standing, Praveen took pre-mature retirement from the Navy to build his financial future through investing in Real Estate. The decision to educate on financial matters paid off, and today he and his wife are comfortably retired on six-figure passive income.

His aim is to help others create wealth in an enlightened way and empower them to live a healthy and happy life. He dedicates his time to write books and articles on financial and spiritual matters.

Prashant graduated with distinction from Auckland University as a computer engineer and later completed his MBA from the world's leading institution - INSEAD. During his successful corporate career, he worked for the most reputable consulting firms in the world - BCG & Deloitte - and represented New Zealand on Prime

Minister-led trade missions to South East Asian countries.

After successfully generating income through his passive investments in property and stocks, Prashant decided to team up with his father to help people transform their lives through the leverage of financial education.

Their website http://wealth-creation-academy.com/ is devoted to teaching people how to create Multiple Streams of Passive Income through investing in real estate, online marketing and creating digital products

Made in the USA
Las Vegas, NV
03 April 2022